ACADIA NATIONAL PARK
Maine's Intimate Parkland

Photographs and Text by Alan Nyiri

Down East Books
Camden, Maine

When I was a small boy, my greatest joy was to walk in the woods with my dad, a pleasure I now share with my own children.

This book is lovingly dedicated to the memory of my Mom and Dad, who introduced me to the woods and shores of Maine; and to my children, Beth and John, who share my love of nature.

Composition and printing
by Argentofot 7238 Oberndorf/N., W. Germany

5 4 3 2

Down East Books, div. of Down East Enterprise, Inc.
Camden, Maine

Contents

Introduction   5

1   Along the Shore   6

2   Across the Mountains   30

3   Through the Forest   50

4   Around the Islands   68

Spruce tree and cliffs in fog.

Introduction

If you drive north along America's east coast, you'll observe that the sand beaches cushioning most of the shore change character some hundred miles beyond Boston. Rocks appear, at first in isolated clusters, punctuating the smooth expanse. Gradually, as you continue northward, the sand is replaced entirely by rock—and you'll know, even without consulting a road map, that you're in Maine. Follow that celebrated rugged coastline, and eventually you'll see granite hills rising above the sea. This uplifting of coastal land culminates on Mount Desert Island, where Cadillac Mountain swells 1530 feet above the Atlantic. You have reached the end of your journey, for this is the land of Acadia, that special place in Maine where nature's forces meet to create an island parkland of singular and haunting beauty.

Acadia's particular charm is derived, in part, from the merging of one environment with another. Where wave meets rock a rich web of life has evolved, composed of organisms that not only endure, but thrive in the inhospitable conditions. Where sea meets mountain, sheer cliffs are created in some places, cobble beaches in others. And just inland from the coastline, marsh, meadow, and forest intertwine. As the land rises, barren outcroppings of rock appear, which, at higher altitudes, reduce forest and meadow to isolated islands of life. To this diversity of environments the atmosphere contributes an infinite variety of moods: rain and sun, fog and haze, ice, snow, and wind interact with the forces of sea and land to create an endless pageant of drama and change.

This combination of so many different elements in a relatively small area creates not only a sense of beauty, but also a strong feeling of intimacy. The eye and mind have ample opportunity to enjoy sweeping panoramas of bay, mountain, and ocean, yet there is something compelling about the landscape that always draws attention back from the grand to the exquisitely minute, creating a balance. I have seen visitors in other national parks, such as the Grand Canyon or Monument Valley, who are overwhelmed by the huge scale in which nature sometimes works its wonders. Becoming very uncomfortable, must they sometimes retreat to the familiar confines of their cars. Of course, this uneasiness prevents the visitor from truly experiencing the park—but, with time and experience, it can usually be overcome.

However, this shrinking from nature doesn't seem to occur at Acadia. Carved on a scale that is comprehensible to everyone and not at all threatening, Acadia seems to embrace and assimilate its visitors. People who announce firmly that they are not "outdoor types" and will go no further than the overlook parking lot are later seen scrambling across the Otter Cliffs, beachcombing the mudflats of Otter Cove, or hiking along Cadillac Mountain's trails — and loving every minute of it. Acadia invites — in fact, almost demands — the participation of its visitors.

For those of us who seek this experience of sharing with nature, Acadia offers special moments to treasure. One day, while photographing along the Ocean Drive cliffs during a dense fog, I happened upon a gem of a scene: a small spruce grew alone at a cliff's edge, veiled in glistening spider webs and skirted with blue harebell. I set up my camera and waited for the shifting mists to part and reveal a glimpse of the nearby cliffs. Suddenly, an unusually large swell crashed against the cliffs, and a small chunk of rock splashed into the sea. Admittedly, this was a small and not uncommon occurrence, yet for me it crystallized the Acadia experience, demonstrating the forces that daily rearrange the structure of Mount Desert Island. In the words of a Park Ranger I once met in the Grand Canyon, Acadia "happened" to me in that moment.

Others may discover the essence of Acadia while picking blueberries on Cadillac Mountain, or watching the fog creep into Frenchman's Bay. The important point is that for most visitors, Acadia *will* somehow, at some time, stimulate this sense of participation and involvement. While this book is not intended as either a travel guide or a nature guide, I sincerely hope it will help to make Acadia "happen" again and again for those who know and love equally its most impressive vistas and tiniest treasures. I also hope it may encourage those who have not yet shared in the Acadia National Park experience to do so, for this most intimate parkland deserves to be explored over and over again.

Along the Shore

A thick mantle of fog swirls soundlessly around me, absorbing the murmur of distant surf and enveloping me in a cool, moist silence. Still I sense the presence of the ocean, a mile away; perhaps I *feel* more than hear its steady rhythm. The familiar, sweet call of a white-throated sparrow pierces the hush briefly; then, with a fluttering of wings it's gone, and the stillness returns. As my trail approaches the Otter Cliffs, a sea breeze rustles the leaves of a nearby maple, and again, for a moment, the silence is gently broken. With the quiet and the fog limiting both vision and hearing, my mind tries to compensate by heightening the sense of smell. I become very aware of the intermingling of forest and ocean scents: the fragrance of balsam fir and the odor of decaying vegetation mix with the delicate aroma of crowberry and the pungence of salt water. Now the drone of a foghorn penetrates the edge of perception; I must be nearing the sea. As I move quickly along the trail, the foghorn's ever-louder warning informs me of my progress.

Emerging from the trees onto the open rocks of the coast, I can barely see the water's edge, only yards away. But the rhythmic breaking of waves along the rocks creates a pleasant, secure feeling, counterbalancing the melancholy mood created by the fog. I enter a small glade at the forest's border, where clusters of brilliant red bunchberries punctuate the greenness. I'm focusing my camera on the nearby ledges when suddenly the fog begins to dissipate; it lingers awhile longer, then lifts altogether. Now I can see back to Sand Beach and Great Head, while beyond the lighthouse on Egg Rock appears to float upon a sea of receding fog. Yet, as magically and mysteriously as it disappeared, only minutes later the cold fog blows back in from the ocean, enshrouding me again, and my attention is once more directed to the objects at my feet.

It is in such foggy times that Acadia unveils its most intimate face to those who don't condemn this as "bad" weather and will venture out to explore. These moments help set the tone and mood of the park and create a sense of intimacy that continues even after sunny weather allows the eye to seek more distant vistas.

Any place where the land confronts the ocean must be an environment of dynamic change. The Acadian coastline is a particularly dramatic example of the ancient combat of land and sea. The stubborn, rocky coast yields only grudgingly to the steady onslaught of the sea – yet it *must* eventually yield. In some places, granite cliffs directly challenge the ocean. Here, while the brutal hammering of storm waves takes its toll on the cliffs, more subtle forces are also at work. Water from rain, frost, and melting snow freezes in cracks on frigid nights; the ice then acts like a sculptor's chisel, inexorably exerting pressure on a chunk of rock until it breaks loose. Even the air can become the cliff's enemy: pounding storm surf may compress air trapped in crevices to rock-splitting force. Similar processes take place, more gradually but just as inevitably, where the land slopes more gently to the sea. In sheltered coves beaches are established when rock fragments, large and small, are tumbled by the waves and worn against each other until they become polished cobbles.

A visit to one of these cobble beaches is a fascinating adventure. My favorite is the beach at Hunter's Cove. While descending the wooden stairway leading from the road down to the beach, you'll notice immediately a barrier of cobbles well back from the water. Winter storm surf has built this sharply sloping ridge, many feet deep. As you walk over this seawall, you hear a distinctive sound; the cobbles rubbing together beneath your feet create an unusual, hollow clatter that echoes between and around the stones. Large waves also roll thousands of these cobbles over and over each other, producing a unique and delightful melody.

A wide variety of cobbles can be found at Hunter's Beach because the cove is situated at the confluence of several different strata of rock. They range in size from a thumbnail to a bathtub, and the color variations are equally diverse. Pink, coarse-grained granite fragments tend to wear down to spherical cobbles. Blue-gray dionite fragments have a tendency to chip off from the bedrock and eventually become smooth, oblong cobbles. Metamorphosed sedimentary rocks of the Bar Harbor series cleave into shingles and form flat cobbles of dark gray, tan, or even green.

I took a break while photographing at Hunter's Cove one day, sitting on a boulder at the water's edge to wait for the tide to recede a bit. A young man and his mother happened by as I was idly tossing cobbles into the water, and we struck up a conversation. He was an engineer by profession, and they vacationed here every year. She was gathering "wishing stones": small cobbles with a layer of quartz running through them, suggesting a white ring around the stone. Offering me one, she explained that to make a wishing stone work, I must grasp it firmly in my hand while making the wish and then immediately toss it into a body of moving water. The ocean would certainly do.

Her son returned each year on a more particular quest. His goal was to find the "perfect" cobble, as round as a rock could be. As he confided this to me I suddenly shot a glance at the ring of ripples where I had just tossed a stone, then turned back to him with an *oh, no!* expression on my face. He must have believed – at least for a second – that I had just flipped his long-sought-after prize into the water, for he took a hesitant step in that direction. But sensing my ruse almost immediately he stopped, and we shared a good laugh.

Whether one seeks a perfect cobble, a perfect photograph, or a perfect moment of peace, Acadia offers its visitors the possibility of fulfilling their ambitions. And as with most such goals, the reward is usually found more in the seeking than in the actual discovery. Still, I sincerely hope that the young engineer finds his perfect cobble someday. Meanwhile, I'll toss a wishing stone in the sea for him.

Cobble beach on Bar Island.

Sunrise at Otter Cliffs (above) overlays the pink granite with a fiery golden glow. A seaside goldenrod (left) has stubbornly staked out its territory in a tiny crack in the granite.

Cliff details near Thunder Hole. The action of water, both from the sea and above, can clearly be seen here as it slowly but unceasingly tears away at the cliff (right). At low tide (below) the results of eons of this action are evident — angular granite fragments have been tossed, ground, and rolled over until they form rounded boulders and cobbles.

Life clings tenaciously to the rocks in the intertidal zone. Barnacles and blue mussels (left) smother the rocks in their abundance. Near Sand Beach (below) rockweed and barnacles add contrast and design to the deep pink granite.

Sand Beach is the largest beach on Mount Desert Island and one of the largest on the Maine Coast north of Portland. The sand here contains an unusually high percentage of carbonaceous material – fragments of clam, mussel, and sea urchin shell, which have the annoying habit of clinging tenaciously to your skin.

Wave action is as varied as the sea itself. Like snowflakes, no two waves are identical. As the tide comes in at Otter Point (below) even moderate surf can create dramatic plumes of spray. Around the point in Otter Cove (left), the wave action is more gentle. Cadillac Mountain rises in the distance.

Common beach grass grows along the mudflats in Otter Cove (right), intertwined with beach pea. In an estuary such as the one at Thomas Bay (below), sea grasses make up the bulk of the biomass that fuels an enormously rich and productive ecosystem.

A study of contrasting coastal rocks. At left, the cliffs near Thunder Hole are rimmed by a beach of wave-worn boulders. A more gently sloping rock shore (above) is found along the coast at Western Point.

Water tumbles from Man of War Brook at Somes Sound (above). This was one of the few places where early sailing ships could fill their water barrels without sending a longboat far inland. Across the sound, the forest meets the water (right) in a jumble of rocks.

Rockweed finds anchorage in a small protective inlet near Thunder Hole (above) and along the eastern shore of Somes Sound (left). This algae spends about half its life out of water and shelters a great abundance of organisms under its thick, wet mat during low tide.

Moonrise over Mount Desert Island. What could possibly be said about moments like these? Perhaps it's best simply to point out that Egg Rock Lighthouse can be seen on the horizon.

Across the Mountains

Most visitors to Acadia National Park eventually find their way up the spiral road to the summit of Cadillac Mountain. Initially it's the promise of a spectacular view that draws them ever upward: the panorama of surrounding bays and ocean, islands and coastline, and the nearby mountains and lakes is truly magnificent. The summit is also the natural vantage point for viewing a sunrise or sunset, and as each day draws to a close the parking lot is usually full. Once up here, however, this windswept granite dome almost compels you to start exploring. Bare rock ledges invite you to meander through a maze of miniature gardens, isolated on islands of shallow soil. You could easily spend a day or even a week up here, exploring all the nooks and crannies, discovering new vistas from out-of-the-way vantage points, watching hawks and falcons soar, or examining the unusual plant life.

The trees that grow in these tiny plots of earth are particularly interesting. The mountain is a harsh environment that demands special adaptations for survival. The sparse soil in these shallow depressions, and the fierce competition of many species for the limited nutrients available, severely reduce the level of growth any plant can maintain. Trees adapt to this condition of finite space and nutrients by growing more slowly and less vigorously, creating a forest of dwarfed but fully mature trees. It's not uncommon to find a "fully grown" spruce existing in only one cubic yard of soil. Although only four feet high, the tree has nonetheless reached its full growth potential, and may well be over a hundred years old. This same tree, given the better soil and sheltered conditions of the valley below, might have grown ten, twenty, or even thirty times larger.

This compact growth pattern is also an adaptation to the brutal winter weather (which is perhaps an even greater limiting factor than soil conditions). By growing low, and spreading out along the sheltering ground instead of stretching upward to the open sky, the tree improves its chances for survival. When a leader shoot does try to grow straight up, the fierce winds will more than likely tear off all but the strongest branches, or kill the terminal leader outright. Thousands of firs and spruces dot the mountainsides, many with a dense mat of living branches surrounding a thick, stunted trunk from which a bleached, skeletal leader rises for several feet. The overall effect would fascinate a bonsai grower, for it is, in fact, just such examples of mature but dwarfed trees — survivors of a hundred storms — which inspired the ancient art of bonsai.

Struck by the understated beauty and tenacity for life of such trees, Japanese gardeners attempted to duplicate these qualities through careful cultivation. By confining the tree in a container and pruning its roots, the bonsai grower induces slow growth. The stark harmony that nature achieves by wind-pruning all but the strongest branches is emulated by the bonsai artist; using shears to shape the foliage and wire to mold the branches, he creates a living sculpture, replicating through artifice the appearance and aesthetic appeal of these ancient survivors of the wild. Any bonsai enthusiast will discover a new understanding of the origins of his art in these mountains.

Whether one is hiking across the mountains or along the coast, bare rock is the essential foundation of the experience. It is hard to spend more than a day in Acadia without wondering about the origin and history of all this rock. Unlike many other areas in the east where the underlying bedrock is concealed by a layer of soil and vegetation, the geology of Acadia is laid bare for all who are curious to examine.

The Porcupine Islands from Cadillac Mountain.

The oldest visible rocks of Acadia, a bed of schists and gneisses metamorphosed from the sedimentary rock, were formed about 450 million years ago. Named the Ellsworth Formation, this is the first of three distinct sedimentary strata created over the following 75 million years. Next is the Cranberry Island Series, a level of volcanic tuff formed by the compression of thick deposits of volcanic ash. Finally, millions of years later, the layer of siltstones and conglomerates that we call the Bar Harbor Series was deposited over the earlier courses.

Then, beginning some 375 million years ago, three major magmatic invasions occurred deep beneath the earth's crust. Dionitic and granitic magma, under tremendous pressure, was squeezed up from deep within the core of the earth and injected between the cracks of the overlying sedimentary strata. The final great irruption created a huge granite dome many miles across, buried thousands of feet below the surface. Two hundred million years of alternating eras of erosion and deposition at the earth's surface followed before this formation, the basis for what would become Mount Desert Island, was at last uncovered.

The apex of this huge dome emerged as an unbroken granite mountain, running east and west. Erosion had little effect on the formation for many millions of years; it was not until the most recent geological period of glaciation that this mountain range was appreciably changed.

Then, about 20,000 years ago, the mammoth glacier that had consumed most of Canada began advancing through that northeast area we now know as New England. It proceeded, slowly but without incident, until it encountered a granite giant, that Mount Desert Island range, laying perpendicular to its path. Although stopped and diverted for a time, the irresistible glacier eventually forced its way over the mountains. With the power of billions of tons of frozen snow the mile-thick ice sheet cut, chiseled, and gouged its way through the mountains. Taking advantage of every small valley or tiny declivity that allowed it to obtain a firmer grip, the glacier inexorably advanced up the northern slopes of the hills and mountains, grinding, smoothing, and polishing the existing landforms into the gradual slopes seen today. Spilling more swiftly down the southern face of the mountains, the glacier plucked huge chunks of rock from the surface and dug deeply into existing fractures, creating sheer cliffs.

When the ice sheet finally retreated, it left behind a series of north-south trending ridges separated by wide, U-shaped valleys. Many of these troughs and valleys later filled with water to become lakes and ponds. One particularly deep trough filled with seawater to become the east coast's only true fjord, Somes Sound.

The glacier's tremendous weight had another effect on the earth's crust: the land beneath it was depressed at least six hundred feet. But when the ice sheet finally slowed, halted, and retreated — about 13,000 years ago — the land started to rebound. And as it rose, so did the sea level. The glacier had locked up a significant portion of the planet's water, causing the sea level to drop drastically during this period; now, as the ice melted, the sea level rose even faster than the land could recover. Thus when the rising land stabilized, about 9,500 years ago, many of the deeper valleys were still flooded by the ocean, creating the "drowned coast" we know today.

And the changes continue: bit by bit, stone by boulder, Acadia is still being eroded, shifted, transformed. This transformation will continue for millions of years, until our beloved park is unrecognizable. But that's a long way down the road — perhaps longer than man will tread.

A mountain rock garden.

Sheep laurel grows profusely around the rocks of the highlands. Beautiful gray, blue-gray and yellow-green lichens begin the disintegration process on these granite fragments (above). Rain approaches from beyond the Cranberry Islands in this view from the south face of Cadillac Mountain, at left.

Balanced Rock, an erratic deposited here by the last glacier, seems ready to tumble off the South Bubble (right). A short hike away, spectacular views of Jordan Pond are found from North Bubble, here blooming with sheep laurel (below).

As I photographed patterns of lichen and other plants that exploit every crevice (left), a garter snake came forward to offer its modeling services (below).

Eagle Lake appears as a pool of liquid sapphire from the north ridge of North Bubble (above). High above Echo Lake, a beech tree (right) in autumn dress nestles among the rocks of Beach Cliff.

Birch trees, well adapted to life in poor, thin soil, thrive on the lower mountain slopes. A yellow birch (left) grows along the trail up the Precipice, while a stand of white birch (below) graces the slopes of the Beehive. Glacial plucking accounts for the steep cliffs on this mountain.

Black huckleberry, which grows in abundance all over the mountains of Acadia National Park, turns a brilliant scarlet in the autumn season (below). At right, a mountain freshet flows for only a day following a hard summer rain. The mountains literally drip after such a storm, as the rain runs off the bare granite slopes.

Trees find existence a struggle on the mountain. A red spruce (above) has had all but its lowest branches stripped off by the fierce winter storms. A solitary pitch pine (left) takes a stand against the weather on the upper reaches of Cadillac Mountain.

Acadia is the ideal place for the inveterate cloud watcher. High cirrus clouds add interest to a sunrise climb up the Precipice (right) on Champlain Mountain. Morning fog (below) pours into Frenchman's Bay from the ocean, passing through the valleys and over the mountains.

Through the Forest

While some visitors come to Acadia to enjoy the rugged coastline, and others are drawn by the unique mountains, many people I've talked with find the heart and soul of *their* Acadia deep in its forests. Alongside the spruce and fir, pine and hardwoods, a special kind of magic is also rooted, a distinctive, intimate bond that has marked man's relationship with trees from prehistoric times. Providers of shelter, warmth, food, and clothing — it's no wonder that so many human cultures have revered trees!

In the Acadian forest, vast biological regions overlap. Arctic species, such as white spruce and crowberry, grow in close proximity to pitch pine and other southern coastal varieties. This rich diversity of northern and temperate species creates a forest complex delightful to both the eye and the mind.

Many different types of forest grow on Acadia, and if you wander anywhere across the island for a few miles, you're almost sure to pass through several of them. But take time for a little bit of planning before you set out; this will enable you to cover the maximum of arboreal territory with minimum wear on your hiking boots.

One of my favorite trails lies along the western shore of Jordan Pond, continuing on up to the summits of the Bubbles. This route takes one through just about every type of forest growing on Acadia, yet is short enough to complete in an afternoon. Starting at the southern end of the pond, near the Jordan Pond House, you cross Jordan Stream to reach the trailhead. The path winds along the shore through a dense forest where red spruce predominates — although a watchful eye will discern other species growing here also. An occasional white pine towers aloofly among the spruces, while chickadees flit from branch to branch and a nuthatch creeps along its trunk; a spicy perfume reveals the presence of a few balsam firs nearby.

As you continue along beside the pond, you may catch sight of a loon diving for fish and bobbing up again. Better yet, you may get to hear one call: no sound on earth matches the liquid, ululating cry of a loon, echoing off the cliffs — an incantation that seems to distill the pure mystique of Maine's North Woods into sound.

You may also come upon a belted kingfisher along this shore, perhaps perched on a dead limb overhanging the pond, or hovering over the water preparing to dive. The kingfisher's diving abilities are matched only by the osprey's, and if you're really lucky you may see one of these fish hawks circling in search of prey. When it spots a trout or salmon near the surface, the osprey will suddenly bank, turn, and dive straight at the water, usually to rise instantly, its arc of flight unbroken — but with the fish clutched in its talons. This powerful bird is capable of capturing fish of heroic size, and to watch one accomplish the feat is a sight never to be forgotten.

Moving back into the forest, you pass through several bogs — cool, swampy places where northern white cedar abound, as well as eastern hemlock and an occasional red maple. Animal life in plentiful here also. Keep an eye peeled for a white-tailed deer; the cedar bog is one of their favorite haunts. And you may encounter a porcupine lumbering about, although the chances of

Cinnamon fern in a moss garden.

spying one are greater if you lift your glance aloft: they're more likely to be high in the treetops, munching on tender buds and bark. You'll almost certainly see red squirrels and chipmunks scampering about, but most of the other creatures of these woods – raccoons, skunks, weasels, minks, foxes, hares, and flying squirrels – are nocturnal feeders, rarely seen during the day.

Along the shore, and in the streams and pools, many other creatures make their homes. Green frogs, pickerel frogs, bullfrogs, and peepers – there are frogs everywhere you look. Salamanders are common in the woods, and turtles may be observed sunning themselves on logs or rocks.

Reaching the northern end of Jordan Pond, you'll find a large marshy area, created partly by the natural lay of the land and partly by beaver dams, which supports a rich variety of life here at the base of the Bubbles. Along the stream that enters the pond grow alder and aspen, birch, swamp and red maple, shadbush, a few black spruce, larch, and rhodora. The colorful display these trees put on in the fall is dazzling.

If you plan to ascend the Bubbles, be warned that the trail climbs steeply. Fortunately, however, the climb quickly ends, for the Bubbles rise no more than 500 feet above the level of Jordan Pond. On the way up, you'll pass through yet another area of mixed hardwoods: a small oak/beech forest blends into another of mountain maple and quaking aspen. It was here that I saw my first pileated woodpecker.

I was resting on a log when a large, crow-sized bird flew overhead, landing on the dead branch of a nearby tree. I knew what it was almost immediately; no other woodpecker in these woods has the flame-red crest, large dark bill, and black-and-white striped neck that make this species instantly identifiable. This extremely shy bird is rarely seen, but it can often be heard deep in the forest hammering large cavities in dead wood, searching for insects. As this one gouged a hole in the limb, wood chips flew everywhere. Finally, with a loud croak, it flew off, leaving me spellbound.

As one approaches the summit of the Bubbles, pitch pine dominate the craggy slopes. At their northern limit here, they do not grow in the usual tapered, triangular shape of many conifers. Instead, their asymmetrical branches form abstract patterns of oriental grace, suggesting the look of a Japanese tea garden. Gray birch also struggle to grow up here, often in soil so poor that the trees remain stunted throughout their short lives.

However, many shrubs thrive along the high ridges, forming a significant part of the upland forest community. Dwarf juniper grows in low, dense mats, often successfully homesteading a crevice where less hardy plants have been unable to survive. Black crowberry, an arctic evergreen shrub, grows in damp depressions on high ridges, as do Labrador tea and black huckleberry. Sheep laurel seems to spring up everywhere here, and in July its pink flowers are a rosy contrast to its attractive – but poisonous – summer greenery.

The forest hike I've described is, of course, only one of a number of possibilities. I'm sure that as you explore the island you'll discover your own favorite trails, and perhaps you too will discover that the heart of *your* Acadia lies in one particular little patch of woods.

A mountain stream colored by autumn foliage.

Eagle Lake is surrounded by color in October. An excellent example of a typically U-shaped valley created by the glacier can be seen between Cadillac and Pemetic mountains (below).

Sphagnum moss carpets the floor of this cedar bog along Man of War Brook (above). Bunchberry, wild lily-of-the-valley, starflower, and various mosses surround a clump of orange Clitocybe mushrooms (right).

Beavers have created a huge marshy area in Great Meadow. Bladderwort speckles the surface of a small pool with pinpoints of yellow (left). Winterberry adds a splash of autumn color to the Marsh (below).

Peace and stillness pervade this birch forest on an early July morning (below). Bunchberries (right) are a member of the Dogwood family. They grow abundantly in cool forest clearings.

Jordan Pond is famous for its clear, cold waters, its restaurant, and its view of the Bubbles. This twilight view of these hills from the south shore (left) shows them as most visitors see them. A more oblique view from the northwest end of the lake (above) shows the gradual north slopes carved by the glacier.

Roots weave interesting patterns on the forest floor. A yellow birch (right) creates a web of roots across a stream bank. Above, buttresslike roots support a massive maple.

Many non-native wild plants flourish in Acadia's climate and environment. Wild lupines (left), brought in from the Pacific Northwest , are common throughout much of Maine. The ubiquitous apple tree (below) marks the site of an earlier homestead.

Around the Islands

Numerous islands dot the waters of the Mount Desert Island region. They are the remnants of ancient hilltops, proof of the "drowned coast" condition of this shoreline in which ancient valleys were flooded by the rising ocean, leaving only the high ground above water. Three islands or island groups are included in Acadia National Park. Most familiar are the Porcupine Islands in Frenchman's Bay, off the northeastern shore of Bar Harbor. The Cranberry Islands lie off the southern coast of Mount Desert, but only part of Baker Island is actually included within the park boundaries. And finally, about twenty-five miles to the southwest of Mount Desert Island, far out in the Atlantic, rises the queen of the offshore islands: Isle au Haut. Although the islands of each group are similar in nature each has its own distinct personality and is, in essence, a miniature Acadia, with its own shore, forest, and highland areas.

The most accessible is Bar Island, which is connected to Bar Harbor by a gravel bar, giving it and the town their names. At low tide you can walk across the bar to the island and enjoy a true island experience. The southern shore is composed mostly of gravel, with, farther on, a jumble of large boulders. These give way to high cliffs along the southeastern end of the island. From here you get excellent views of Bar Harbor, Frenchman's Bay, and the other two park islands, Sheep Porcupine and Bald Porcupine. A lovely cobble beach at the base of the cliffs may cause one to lose all sense of time while exploring for interesting rocks, but beware! If you forget to cross back over the connecting bar before the tide comes in you'll be stranded for the next twelve hours.

Bald Porcupine and Sheep Porcupine islands are accessible only by boat, and I spent a delightful day cruising around the bay and these islands in a rented craft. But unfortunately, landing on either of the Porcupines is tricky, and the boat-rental company would not allow it. Instead, I contented myself with exploring their shores from the water with camera and binoculars. The view of Mount Desert Island from Frenchman's Bay is wonderful, affording a unique perspective on the park, and I saw many other people enjoying this vista from the decks of pleasure schooners sailing the bay.

Marine life in the bay is plentiful. As I cruised near one island, I disturbed a few harbor seals sunning on the rocks. In fact, I encountered many seals around the bay that day; as I drifted near the islands, making photographs, often seals would pop their heads up nearby, as if to see what I was doing.

I also saw numerous groups of Atlantic harbor porpoises, leaping playfully from the water in graceful arcs — or perhaps I only saw the same group numerous times. I would have liked to get some pictures of them, but they were always too far away. Finally, while drifting near Burnt Porcupine Island, I got my chance. My attention was focused on the image in my viewfinder when suddenly five porpoises surfaced, surrounding the boat, and blew their spouts in unison. The terrific *whoosh!* they created was so loud, and its effect so startling, that I almost dropped my camera overboard — only the neckstrap saved it. I whirled this way and that, trying to get a picture of one, but each porpoise disappeared as I aimed the camera in its direction — and soon, all were gone. They reappeared only once, some time and distance away, and emitted an unusual

Dawn illuminates the Porcupine Islands in Frenchman's Bay just east of Bar Harbor. From left to right are: Sheep Porcupine, Burnt Porcupine, Long Porcupine, and Bald Porcupine. Not visible is Bar Island to the left of Sheep Porcupine.

sound. Now, I'll never be able to prove it, but I could swear they were laughing.

Soon after this, I spotted a pair of nesting bald eagles on Long Porcupine Island. While I know this magnificent bird is making a comeback along the coast, these were the first eagles I'd seen in many years. It felt wonderful to have firsthand proof of their return, but I moved away quickly lest I disturb them.

An adventure to Isle au Haut begins with an early-morning trip on the mailboat. After a peaceful 45-minute cruise among the offshore islands, the mailboat arrives at the village landing on the northwest tip of the island. That end of Isle au Haut is still privately owned, while the southwestern two-thirds belong to the National Park Service. Allowed to exist in a natural state since 1943, and in fact little used for the past eighty years, the park area now has the feeling of a true wilderness. And, as in any wilderness, access to this part of the island is limited. Visitors are restricted to the capacity of the mailboat, on a first-come, first-served basis. Camping is limited to a few sites, obtainable by reservation only, and no amenities of civilization — plumbing, electricity, telephone — are provided.

It's a 5½-mile hike from the town landing to the spectacular coastline of the island's southwestern shore — a pleasant morning's walk along the Duck Harbor Trail. This path winds through the island's heavily wooded interior, and then skirts the coast around Moore's Harbor. The inland portion of the trail takes you through numerous bogs and marshes, and the footing is often quite wet. Few clues indicate that you're on an island here; the forest appears like any other. I even startled a great eight-point buck in a cedar bog — or rather,he startled me. I don't believe either of us expected to see the other, but I came around a boulder and there he stood, square in the middle of the path. For a split second I thought he might run me over in his flight, but after taking one bound toward me he cut to his right and disappeared into the dense foliage.

After passing Duck Harbor, where the mailboat makes noon and evening stops, a short hike of about another mile brings you to the south shore. Here, several cobble beaches offer idyllic spots for a picnic. I found that a leisurely afternoon hike along Western Head Trail provided excellent views of both the island coast and the vast expanse of the Atlantic. This, I felt, was a truly remote, unspoiled area. The spruce forest seemed ancient, primitive, and somewhat eerie, even in sunny midsummer; I imagine that on a cold, foggy day it might seem haunted. Perhaps it is.

I arrived back at the Duck Harbor landing in plenty of time to meet the evening mailboat, tired from hiking eleven miles carrying my heavy camera pack, yet exhilarated by the day's experiences.

A trip to Isle au Haut is a most rewarding adventure, but then so is any encounter with the many delights offered by Acadia National Park. Here each visitor has a unique opportunity to explore nature on a personal level and discover among the many wonders, presented on a scale ranging from the miniature to the grandiose, the one special quality that ever after will define the park. Let Acadia "happen" to you, and share in the care and preservation of this magnificent environment — Maine's intimate parkland.

The western tip of the Hop, a small island at the northeast end of Long Porcupine Island.

Sheer cliffs of diorite rise almost vertically from the water on the southeast end of Bald Porcupine Island. Lichens and mineral stains create the effect of a painter's palette.

Bald Porcupine Island sets majestically in the placid waters of Frenchman's Bay. Champlain Mountain appears on the horizon.

Deep Cove, on Isle au Haut's southern coast, is rimmed by a broad cobble beach (right), and backed by a high cobble seawall (below).

The coast of Isle au Haut is very irregular (left), with many small coves and inlets. The rock along this coast (above) is a blend of volcanic formations – felsite, breccia, and volcanic tuff.

Volcanic rock along the southern coast of Isle au Haut fractures and erodes differently from the bedrock on Mount Desert Island. The effect is reminiscent of a Mediterranean coast.

The Photographs and the Photographer

Alan Nyiri lives in mid-state New York, but spends more than half of each year traveling about the United States visiting, on an average, forty college campuses, where he creates "campus landscapes" for full-color postcards, note cards and prints.

He also makes it a point to visit at least three national parks each year in his travels, and here he does the major share of his personal photography.

His winters are spent visiting with his family, printing in his Oneonta, New York darkroom, and doing those other everyday tasks that are part of daily living.

All but a few of the photographs in this book were made with a 4x5 Toyo view camera, using 75mm and 90mm Nikkor lenses, and 135mm and 210mm Schneider optics. The exceptions are several photographs in the "Islands" chapter, which were made with a 2¼ x 2¼ Hasselblad. His usual lenses are Nikkor 75mm and 90mm, and Schneider 135mm and 210mm.

Back cover: Bass Harbor Head Lighthouse